"BRING THE CLASSICS TO LIFE"

The Adventures of Huckleberry Finn

LEVEL 1

Series Designer
Philip J. Solimene

Editor
Laura M. Solimene

EDCON

Long Island, New York

Story Adapter
Donna B. Wilson

Author
Mark Twain

About the Author

In a small Missouri town in the year 1835, Mark Twain was born Samuel Langhorn Clemens. As a young man, he piloted river steamers along the Mississippi River. Later, he began to write short stories for newspapers. Some of his novels include, *A Connecticut Yankee in King Arthur's Court, Life on the Mississippi,* and *The Prince and the Pauper.* His novels, *The Adventures of Tom Sawyer* and *The Adventures of Huckleberry Finn* reflect many of his own boyhood experiences.

Copyright © 2008
A/V Concepts Corp.
Edcon Publishing

info@edconpublishing.com
1-888-553-3266   Fax 1-888-518-1564
30 Montauk Blvd. Oakdale NY 11769
www.edconpublishing.com

Printed in U.S.A.
10 ISBN #1-55576-0880
13 ISBN #9-781555-760885

CONTENTS

Words Used 4, 5

TEACHER'S NOTE

In adapting this classic, we have tried to maintain the 'flavor' of the original as much as possible, therefore, we have added a special section entitled, "Slang of the Day." This will aid the reader in understanding some of the words that were commonly used in the South during the mid 1800's.

WORDS USED

Story 41	Story 42	Story 43	Story 44	Story 45
KEY WORDS				
about	got	all	again	came
but	had	children	hand	door
give	him	they	hear	pig
she	his	when	so	some
that	then	woman	who	would
NECESSARY WORDS				
adventure	awful	bedroom	bank	body
meow	awfully	pretend	dirty	broke
rich	blood	really	foot	canoe
robbers	candle	woods	maybe	island
truth	cave		rags	jail
stretch	clothes		stuff	lock
	kitchen			sell
	lot			wife
	river			
	rule			
	slave			
	witch			

WORDS USED

Story 46	Story 47	Story 48	Story 49	Story 50
KEY WORDS				
one	back	bag	as	better
took	boy	bed	being	off
very	just	girl	feet	put
water	other	letter	road	soon
wet	way	uncle	walked	think
NECESSARY WORDS				
care	runaway	coffin	cousin	bullet
fight	rope	end	hug	danger
float	sign	plan	spirit	dig
gun		real	sold	doctor
quiet			townspeople	enough
raft				free
steamboat				rat
				snake
				spider
				steal

Huck and the Widow Douglas

PREPARATION

Key Words

about	(ə bout´)	having to do with *I am reading a book <u>about</u> rock and roll.*
but	(but)	on the other hand *I don't like milk <u>but</u> I'll drink it.*
give	(giv)	hand over, sometimes as a gift *Bob will <u>give</u> me some money for gas.*
she	(shē)	she is used instead of a female's name; her; the girl; the woman *Mary is on the phone. <u>She</u> wants to talk to you.*
that	(THat)	pointing out some person, thing or idea already talked about *I told you about <u>that</u> boy last night.*

Huck and the Widow Douglas

Necessary Words

adventure	(ad ven´chər)	something a person does that is fun and sometimes dangerous *My first trip by train was an adventure.*
cried	(krīd)	past tense of cry *The baby cried at the doctor's yesterday.*
mainly	(mān´lē)	for the most part *That store sells mainly sport shoes.*
meow	(mēou´)	the sound made by a cat or kitten *I found my lost cat when I heard its meow in the tree.*
rich	(rich)	having much money or land *I will be rich if I find the buried treasure.*
robbers	(rob´ərs)	persons who rob or steal; thieves *The robbers took the man's car.*
truth	(trüth)	that which is true; not a lie *Mother told me that I should always tell the truth.*
stretch	(strech)	to say or think something is greater than it is; to go beyond the truth *When Joe said he caught a fish bigger than a whale, he was stretching the truth.*

People

Mark Twain	is the man who wrote THE ADVENTURES OF HUCKLEBERRY FINN and THE ADVENTURES OF TOM SAWYER.
Tom Sawyer	is Huckleberry's good friend.
Aunt Polly	is Tom Sawyer's aunt and Aunt Sally's sister.
Widow Douglas	is the kind woman who takes Huckleberry into her home to care for him.
Judge Thatcher	is the judge who takes care of Huck's money.

Things

THE ADVENTURES OF TOM SAWYER	is a book.
Moses and the Bulrushes	is a story from the Bible.

Huck and the Widow Douglas

Huck tries to be a good boy for the Widow.

Preview: 1. Read the name of the story.
2. Look at the picture.
3. Read the sentence under the picture.
4. Read the first two paragraphs of the story.
5. Then answer the following question.

You learned from your preview that Huck thought that
___ a. the Widow was a nice woman.
___ b. the Widow was not very nice.
___ c. the Widow was rich.
___ d. the Widow would do his schoolwork.

Turn to the Comprehension Check on page 10 for the right answer.

Now read the story.

Read to find out why the Widow had cried.

Huck and the Widow Douglas

Do you know me? I'm Huck Finn. I was in THE ADVENTURES OF TOM SAWYER. That book was made by Mark Twain. He told the truth, mainly. He did stretch some parts. That's nothing. I never heard of people who always told the truth. Well, now that I say that, Aunt Polly and the Widow do. They are in the book, too. The book is mainly the truth. It's made with some stretchers. But I said that before.

Now the book stops when Tom and I get rich. Judge Thatcher keeps the money for us. But he'll give us a little of it any time we want. The Widow said she'd give me a home. She said she'd help me do good with my schooling and such. She was pretty good herself and was nice as could be. I tried to be good.

The Widow liked to keep me in the house most times. A day came when I couldn't take much more. I ran away. I was glad I was rich now. But I was more glad running outside.

Tom Sawyer found me later on. He said he was getting up a game of robbers. He said he'd let me in on it. But I had to go back to the Widow. I went back.

The Widow cried. But she was happy. She gave me some food. But, I didn't get to eat it right away. She said something soft-like over the food. She was always doing that.

She told me a good story. It was about Moses and the Bulrushes. Later, I heard Moses is not around any more. I don't like to know about dead people.

That night I heard a "me-ow! me-ow!" outside. I knew it was Tom Sawyer. It was time for the robber game!

Huck and the Widow Douglas

COMPREHENSION CHECK

Choose the best answer.

1. Huck liked
   ___a. going to school.
   ___b. to read books.
   ___c. to play outside.
   ___d. being good.

2. The Widow Douglas and Aunt Polly
   ___a. made up stories.
   ___b. always told the truth.
   ___c. never told the truth.
   ___d. didn't talk much.

3. In the book THE ADVENTURES OF TOM SAWYER, Huck and Tom
   ___a. get old.
   ___b. get sick.
   ___c. get help.
   ___d. get rich.

4. Tom Sawyer is
   ___a. Huck's good friend.
   ___b. Huck's brother.
   ___c. Huck's father.
   ___d. Huck's uncle.

5. Huck ran away because
   ___a. the Widow did not like him.
   ___b. his friend Tom had run away.
   ___c. he wanted to be alone.
   ___d. it was hard for him to be good all the time.

6. Tom Sawyer talked Huck into
   ___a. going back to the Widow's house.
   ___b. staying out all night.
   ___c. a game of tag.
   ___d. being a good boy.

7. When Huck went back to the Widow, why was she crying?
   ___a. Huck didn't come home for dinner.
   ___b. Huck didn't make his bed.
   ___c. She was happy to see that Huck was okay.
   ___d. She had soap in her eyes.

8. Huck knew it was time for the robber game
   ___a. when dinner was over.
   ___b. when school was over.
   ___c. when it got dark.
   ___d. when he heard "me-ow! me-ow!" outside.

9. Another name for this story could be
   ___a. "Huck and the Robber Game."
   ___b. "A New Home for Huck."
   ___c. "Huck Gets Rich."
   ___d. "Moses and the Bulrushes."

10. This story is mainly about
    ___a. Huck's new life with the Widow Douglas.
    ___b. Huck's friend Tom Sawyer.
    ___c. Tom and Huck getting rich.
    ___d. a book by Mark Twain.

Check your answers with the key on page 67.

Huck and the Widow Douglas

VOCABULARY CHECK

about	but	give	she	that

I. Sentences to Finish

Fill in the blank in each sentence with the correct key word from the box above.

1. Tom will _____ milk to the little kitten.

2. The boy got lost, _____ he didn't cry.

3. I will give the girl some ice cream if _____ is good.

4. Mother said _____ she will make some cookies.

5. Ted will tell us _____ his pet rabbit.

II. Crossword Puzzle

Use the words from the box above to fill in the puzzle. Use the meanings below to help you choose the right answer.

Across

1. having to do with
3. her; that girl; the woman
4. on the other hand

Down

1. hand over, sometimes as a gift
2. pointing out something already talked about

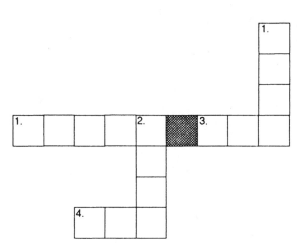

Check your answers with the key on page 69.

This page may be reproduced for classroom use.

Jim and the Witches

PREPARATION

Key Words

got	(got)	past tense of get *Mom <u>got</u> a new dress for her birthday.*
had	(had)	paste tense of have *I <u>had</u> three cookies at lunch today.*
him	(him)	him is used instead of a male's name; that boy; that man *Joe wanted more cake. I gave <u>him</u> some more.*
his	(hiz)	belonging to a boy or a man *Danny brought <u>his</u> ball to the game.*
then	(THen)	1. at that time *The party was over and <u>then</u> we went home.* 2. soon afterwards *I opened the door and <u>then</u> the lights went out.*

Jim and the Witches

Necessary Words

awful/awfully   (ô´ fəl)

       1. very large; great
            Tim is <u>awfully</u> afraid of spiders.
       2. terrible
            The smell of dead fish is <u>awful</u>.

blood   (blud)

       the liquid in the veins of animals with backbones
            Father took some of the horse's <u>blood</u> for a test.

candle   (kan´dl)

       a stick of wax that is used to give light
            When the lights went out, Mother lit a <u>candle</u>.

cave   (kāv)

       a hole under the ground or in the side of a mountain
            The bear left its <u>cave</u> to find some food.

clothes   (klōz)

       cloth used to cover the body
            I will need new <u>clothes</u> for the party.

kitchen   (kich´ən)

       a room where food is cooked
            Mother was making cookies in the <u>kitchen</u>.

lot   (lot)

       many
            There are a <u>lot</u> of cows on Mike's farm.

river   (riv´ər)

       a large stream of water that empties into another body of water
            I took a ride down the <u>river</u> in my new boat.

rule   (rül)

       something that shows us the way to act or not to act
            The <u>rule</u> at this house is to wipe your feet at the door.

slave   (slāv)

       long ago, a person who was owned by another person
            Mr. Ward's <u>slave,</u> Joe, worked very hard and very long.

witch   (wich)

       a woman who is supposed to have magic powers
            The ugly <u>witch</u> eats mice and spiders.

People

Miss Watson   is the Widow's sister. She lives with the Widow and Huck.

Slang of the Day

sumf'n   something
warn't   weren't/were not

Jim and the Witches

"I know I heard sumf'n," said Jim.

Preview: 1. Read the name of the story.
          2. Look at the picture.
          3. Read the sentence under the picture.
          4. Read the first paragraph of the story.
          5. Then answer the following question.

You learned from your preview that Jim went to the window
___ a.   to call Huck inside.
___ b.   to look at the flowers in the garden.
___ c.   to look at the moon.
___ d.   because he heard a noise.

Turn to the Comprehension Check on page 16 for the right answer.

Now read the story.

Read to find out where most of Tom's ideas came from.

Jim and the Witches

I warn't asleep and I had my clothes on. I jumped out of bed and out the window. Tom and I went down to the garden. The garden was next to the kitchen. I made a noise. Miss Watson's big slave, Jim, was in the kitchen. He heard me. He got up and looked outside.

"I know I heard sumf'n," said Jim. He looked long and hard into the dark.

We waited for him to go back in. We waited for him to go to sleep. And in a little while, he did. Then, we got candles from the kitchen. Tom put a little money on the table. It was his thanks for the candles.

Later, Jim told everyone some witches had come in the night.

"The witches gave me money and got the candles," said Jim.

Jim's friends thought Jim told the truth. They looked up to him. Jim began to act pretty big. Tom and I did not let on about the real story.

Three friends waited for us down next to the river. We got in a boat and took off fast. Tom knew where there was a cave. We went to it. In the cave, Tom lit a candle.

"Now we'll be robbers," said Tom. "The rule is you have to write your name down in blood. Writing your name in blood makes this not a game."

We thought the rule was great! On the wall of the cave, we wrote our names in blood. Tom gave us more rules. They were good rules, too. Tom said he got his rules from reading books. Tom is smart about an awful lot of things.

We talked a long time in the cave. Then the sun was coming up. We had to go home.

I got a good going over from old Miss Watson. My good clothes were not clean now. She was going to do her best to make me very sorry for it. She did a good job, too.

Jim and the Witches

COMPREHENSION CHECK

Choose the best answer.

1. Why do you think that Huck was in bed with his clothes on?
   ___a. He was trying to keep warm.
   ___b. He could not find his night clothes.
   ___c. He wanted to be ready to sneak out and meet Tom.
   ___d. He liked to sleep with his clothes on.

2. Miss Watson's big slave, Jim, was sitting in the
   ___a. bedroom.
   ___b. T.V. room.
   ___c. bathroom.
   ___d. kitchen.

3. When Jim heard a noise outside, he
   ___a. got up and looked out the window.
   ___b. lit a candle.
   ___c. ran to his room.
   ___d. looked out the door to see who was there.

4. When Jim went to sleep, Huck and Tom
   ___a. took some money from the kitchen table.
   ___b. took candles from the kitchen.
   ___c. took some food from the kitchen.
   ___d. took off to play a game.

5. What was it that made Jim think that witches had come to the house?
   ___a. He found money on the table where the candles had been.
   ___b. He found a note from the witches.
   ___c. He found a witch's broom in the kitchen.
   ___d. He knew that only witches steal candles.

6. First, Huck and Tom met their friends down by the river. Then, they took off in a boat. Next,
   ___a. they all played the robber game.
   ___b. Tom lit a candle.
   ___c. they all went to Tom's cave.
   ___d. Tom told everyone the rules.

7. In the cave, all the boys
   ___a. put their names in blood on the cave wall.
   ___b. lit their own candle.
   ___c. let Tom read a story from his reading books.
   ___d. made up all their own rules.

8. In the cave, the boys
   ___a. were getting hungry.
   ___b. were getting tired.
   ___c. talked for a long time.
   ___d. fell asleep.

9. Another name for this story could be
   ___a. "Running Away From Home."
   ___b. "Tom's Rules."
   ___c. "Fun When the Sun Goes Down."
   ___d. "The Secret Cave."

10. This story is mainly about
    ___a. how some boys have fun.
    ___b. Tom's many rules.
    ___c. stealing candles.
    ___d. a secret cave.

Check your answers with the key on page 67.

Jim and the Witches

VOCABULARY CHECK

got	had	him	his	then

I. Sentences to Finish

Fill in the blank in each sentence with the correct key word from the box above.

1. Jim _____ a new bike for his birthday.

2. We will eat first, _____ we can play outside.

3. Fred brought _____ dog to school.

4. After Sam ate the cookie, I gave _____ another.

5. I _____ to go to the store to get some milk for the baby.

II. Making Sense of Sentences

Put a check next to YES if the sentence makes sense. Put a check next to NO if the sentence does not make sense.

	YES	NO
1. I <u>then</u> told the story and they waited for me to read.	_____	_____
2. Jill told Nancy to bring <u>his</u> doll to school.	_____	_____
3. Kevin <u>got</u> lost on his way to the game.	_____	_____
4. Sally asked for a drink, so I gave <u>him</u> one.	_____	_____
5. If I <u>had</u> tried real hard, I would have won the race.	_____	_____

Check your answers with the key on page 69.

This page may be reproduced for classroom use.

Playing Robbers

PREPARATION

Key Words

all	(ôl)	everyone; every person *We didn't leave school until <u>all</u> of us were in the car.*
children	(chil´drən)	young boys and girls *The <u>children</u> liked the clowns in the show.*
they	(ŦHā)	persons, animals, things or ideas talked about *The children will have ice cream. <u>They</u> will each have one cone.*
when	(hwen)	at what time *<u>When</u> will the train come in?*
woman	(wum´ən)	an adult female *I spoke to a <u>woman</u> at the bank today.*

Playing Robbers

Necessary Words

bedroom (bed´rüm´) a room to sleep in
Tom's <u>bedroom</u> is full of toy trains.

pretend (pri tend´) make believe
Jack will be the king; I will <u>pretend</u> to be queen.

really (rē´ lē) truly; in fact
It was <u>really</u> raining hard today.

woods (wudz) a large number of growing trees; a forest
We walked through the <u>woods</u> to pick some berries.

People

Pap is Huck's father.

Things

Don Quixote is an adventure book about the hero, Don Quixote.

Sunday School is a place, usually in a church, where children learn about the Bible.

Slang of the Day

di'monds diamonds

saphead being "un-cool"

Playing Robbers

Huck knew that the body found in the river could not be Pap's.
He knew that Pap would show up at any time.

Preview: 1. Read the name of the story.
           2. Look at the picture.
           3. Read the sentences under the picture.
           4. Read the first paragraph of the story.
           5. Then answer the following question.

You learned from your preview that Pap
___ a. was a happy man.
___ b. was an angry man.
___ c. dressed like a woman.
___ d. saw Huck every day.

Turn to the Comprehension Check on page 22 for the right answer.

Now read the story.

Read to find out who was waiting for Huck when he got home.

Playing Robbers

Pap had not come into town for more than a year. That was fine with me. I didn't want to see Pap. He was always angry. He'd let me have it all the time. That's when he could catch me. Most times I'd take to the woods. The people from town said they found Pap dead in the river. Well . . . a man that looked like Pap. They said the man was on his back when they found him. Right away I knew it warn't Pap. Dead men are found face down in the river. Most likely, it was a woman. Most likely, the woman was dressed like a man. But I knew my Pap could show up any time. I wasn't happy about that.

Tom and us played robbers lots of times. Then I stopped. We all did. We didn't really rob people. It was all pretend. Tom Sawyer could pretend about anything.

A day came when we saw a lot of children. They were getting out of Sunday School. Tom said they were rich people. He said they had di'monds. We pretended we were robbers. We all made a lot of noise. We ran down to the children. Then, a Sunday School woman came out. She was angry. She stopped us fast!

Later I told Tom I didn't see any di'monds. He said I was a "sap head." He said I had to read a book. It was about a man, Don Quixote. Then he said I'd learn something.

Tom is really smart and I thought about all he said. But it came down to this. Don Quixote or no Don Quixote, Tom's "rich people" looked too much like children from a Sunday School for the likes of me.

When I got home, Pap was sitting in my bedroom. He was waiting for me.

Playing Robbers

COMPREHENSION CHECK

Choose the best answer.

1. Huck had not seen his pap for
   ___a. three years.
   ___b. two years.
   ✓c. more than a year.
   ___d. ten days.

2. Huck and his friends played the robber game
   ___a. all the time.
   ___b. every day.
   ___c. every Sunday.
   ✓d. many times.

3. The "robber game"
   ✓a. was just a game for "fun."
   ___b. could send the boys to jail.
   ___c. could make the boys rich.
   ___d. never really scared anyone.

4. Tom said the children from Sunday School
   ___a. were giving away di'monds.
   ___b. liked to play the robber game, too.
   ___c. made a lot of noise.
   ✓d. were rich people.

5. The Sunday School woman was angry with the boys
   ✓a. for scaring the children.
   ___b. for not going to church.
   ___c. for taking the di'monds.
   ___d. for making so much noise.

6. Tom called Huck a "sap head" because Huck
   ___a. had a funny-looking head.
   ___b. never read any books.
   ✓c. didn't understand that the di'monds were supposed to be "make believe."
   ___d. scared the children.

7. Because Tom was very "smart,"
   ✓a. the boys looked up to him.
   ___b. the would all be rich someday.
   ___c. he would find real di'monds one day.
   ___d. he was not liked by the other children.

8. When Huck got home, he found his pap
   ___a. sleeping.
   ___b. eating.
   ___c. reading.
   ✓d. waiting for him.

9. Another name for this story could be
   ___a. "A Day at Church."
   ✓b. "Fun and Games."
   ___c. "Sap Heads."
   ___d. "Stealing Di'monds."

10. This story is mainly about
    ___a. finding a dead man in the river.
    ___b. an angry Sunday School woman.
    ___c. Tom and Don Quixote.
    ✓d. some boys who like to "pretend" and have fun.

Check your answers with the key on page 67.

Playing Robbers

VOCABULARY CHECK

all	children	they	when	woman

I. Sentences to Finish

Fill in the blank in each sentence with the correct key word from the box above.

1. The _____ were happy to see Mother making cookies.

2. We _____ went home after the party.

3. John can go out to play _____ it stops raining.

4. The boys went home because _____ were hungry.

5. The old _____ next door gave the boys some pie.

II. Matching

Write the letter of the correct meaning from Column B next to the key word in Column A.

Column A	Column B
____1. all	a. an adult female
____2. children	b. persons, animals, things or ideas talked about
____3. they	c. everyone; every person
____4. when	d. young boys and girls
____5. woman	e. at what time

Check your answers with the key on page 69.

A Visit From Pap

PREPARATION

Key Words

again	(ə gen´)	once more *I got a new piece of paper and wrote the letter <u>again</u>.*
hand	(hand)	the end part of the arm *Hold my <u>hand</u> when we walk across the street.*
hear	(hir)	get sounds through the ear; listen *The judge will <u>hear</u> you now.*
so	(sō)	1. for this reason *I was cold, <u>so</u> I put on my coat.* 2. a sound of surprise *<u>So</u>, I see you've come at last!*
who	(hü)	a word used in asking a question about a person or persons; which person? *<u>Who</u> are you taking to the party?*

A VISIT FROM PAP

Necessary Words

bank   (bangk)   a place for keeping and lending money
         Mike puts money in the <u>bank</u> every week.

dirty   (der´ tē)   not clean
         My hands are <u>dirty</u> because I was working on the motor.

foot   (fu̇t)   the end part of the leg
         Her <u>foot</u> was too big for the shoe.

maybe   (mā´ bē)   perhaps; possibly
         <u>Maybe</u> you'll have better luck next time.

rags   (ragz)   torn cloth
         The dogs ripped the slipper to <u>rags</u>.

stuff   (stuf)   thing or things
         Put your <u>stuff</u> back in the closet.

People

George Washington   first President of the United States

Slang of the Day

ain't   am not; are not; is not

hain't   have not

high-faluttin'   stuck up; snotty

lemme   let me

put on airs   pretend to be better than other people

A VISIT FROM PAP

"Think you're pretty fine stuff, don't you?" asked Pap.

Preview: 1. Read the name of the story.
2. Look at the picture.
3. Read the sentence under the picture.
4. Read the first four paragraphs of the story.
5. Then answer the following question.

You learned from your preview that Huck's father lived
___ a.   well.
___ b.   poorly.
___ c.   better than Huck.
___ d.   like a rich man.

Turn to the Comprehension Check on page 28 for the right answer.

Now read the story.

Read to find out why Pap had come to visit.

A Visit From Pap

Pap didn't look too angry, so I didn't run. Pap looked and smelled awful. His hair was long and dirty. His clothes were dirty rags. His foot was coming out of his shoe. He sat in his rags and looked at me.

Then he said, "Clean Clothes? You walk around like you're pretty fine stuff, don't you?"

"Maybe I am. Maybe I ain't," I said.

"You talk back to me again and you'll catch it! I hear tell you're going to school. No going to school will make you better than your old pap! Who said you could go?"

"The Widow," I said.

"And who told the Widow she could put such high-faluttin' stuff in you?"

"No one told her."

"Well, ain't that nice? I'll tell her a thing, pretending she's your mother or something. Your mother could not read more than me. I will not let you get away with this stuff. You stop going to school, you hear? Or you'll catch it! Now lemme hear you read something."

I took up a book and began to read about George Washington. Pap got angry. He gave the book the back of his hand!

"So, they told me the truth! You *can* read! You better not let me catch you reading again. My hand will give you 'what for' fast. I heard you got money, too."

"I hain't got no money."

"I heard that Judge Thatcher's got it," said Pap.

"No. You ask Judge Thatcher. He will tell you." I was telling the truth. Judge Thatcher has the money in a bank for me.

The next day, Pap went to Judge Thatcher. Judge Thatcher told him to get lost. Pap didn't give up. He said he could make Judge Thatcher give over the money. I, too, didn't give up. I went to school every day.

A VISIT FROM PAP

COMPREHENSION CHECK

Choose the best answer.

1. When Huck found Pap waiting for him, he didn't run because
  ___a. he didn't have any shoes on.
  ___b. he was not supposed to run in the house.
  ___c. he was happy to see his father.
  ___d. he didn't think he was in danger.

2. Huck's father was dressed
  ___a. in his best clothes.
  ___b. in clean rags.
  ___c. in dirty rags.
  ___d. in Huck's clothes.

3. Pap thought Huck was "pretty fine stuff" because
  ___a. he was wearing clean clothes.
  ___b. he had a new haircut.
  ___c. he had on a new hat.
  ___d. he had his own room.

4. Huck talked back to Pap because he knew that
  ___a. Pap wanted him to.
  ___b. Pap would not hurt him when the Widow was around.
  ___c. it would make Pap angry.
  ___d. it would make Pap happy.

5. Pap thought that the Widow was trying to be like Huck's
  ___a. grandmother.
  ___b. best friend.
  ___c. mother.
  ___d. teacher.

6. Pap wanted Huck to read something
  ___a. so he could go to sleep.
  ___b. to see if Huck really knew how to read.
  ___c. because he liked to hear Huck's voice.
  ___d. because he liked to help him with his homework.

7. Pap told Huck that he had to stop
  ___a. reading so fast.
  ___b. telling the truth.
  ___c. going to school.
  ___d. playing with Tom Sawyer.

8. When Huck told Pap that Judge Thatcher had the money in the bank,
  ___a. Pap didn't believe him.
  ___b. Pap took the money from Judge Thatcher.
  ___c. Pap gave Huck the back of his hand.
  ___d. Pap just laughed.

9. Another name for this story could be
  ___a. "Happy Together."
  ___b. "Reading For Father."
  ___c. "Talking Back."
  ___d. "Pap Finds a New Huck."

10. This story is mainly about
  ___a. a man who is only looking out for himself.
  ___b. a loving father.
  ___c. a man who could not read well.
  ___d. going to school every day.

Check your answers with the key on page 67.

A Visit From Pap

VOCABULARY CHECK

again	hand	hear	so	who

I. Sentences to Finish

Fill in the blank in each sentence with the correct key word from the box above.

1. If I play the game_____ , I will play much better.

2. Joe said he didn't know _____ played a trick on him.

3. It was raining Saturday, _____ I didn't go outside.

4. Mother said she didn't _____ who had won the game.

5. My brother closed the car door on my _____ , and now it hurts.

II. Word Search

All the words from the box above are hidden in the puzzle below. They may be written from left to right, or up and down. As you find each word, put a circle around it. One word, that is not a key word, has been done for you.

```
H   Z   P   W   H   O   T   S
E   W   X   X   A   N   O   N
A   G   A   I   N   H   J   A
R   I   B   C   D   K   O   P
G   E   E   V   F   U   S   N
Y   N   G   E   A   R   V   A
S   T   V   F   O   Q   Y   O
O   K   L   L   W   R   X   W
```

Check your answers with the key on page 70.

This page may be reproduced for classroom use.

I Trick Pap and Get Away!

PREPARATION

Key Words

came	(kām)	past tense of come *The mail <u>came</u> early today.*
door	(dôr)	a thing used to open or close the way to a room *Close the <u>door</u> so the flies don't come in!*
pig	(pig)	an animal who is raised for its meat; a young hog *My brother's <u>pig</u> won a prize at the county fair.*

some	(sum)	1. a part of, not all
		    I ate <u>some</u> of the dessert.
		2. any
		    I will ask <u>some</u> person to take me home.

would	(wŭd)	was willing to; past tense of will *I asked Bill if he <u>would</u> bring home some milk.*

I Trick Pap and Get Away!

Necessary Words

body	(bod´ē)	the whole part of a person *Sally's whole <u>body</u> got burned from the sun.*
broke	(brōk)	past tense of break *Tom is sorry that he <u>broke</u> his bike.*
canoe	(kə nü´)	a light boat pointed at both ends and moved with a paddle *The Indians went up the river in their <u>canoe</u>.*
island	(ī´lənd)	some land in the middle of some water *I would love to go to an <u>island</u> and find treasure.*
jail	(jāl)	a place to put people who break the law; a prison *The robber went to <u>jail</u> for holding up the store.*
lock	(lok)	1. a thing that, when put together, cannot be opened without a key. *He put a <u>lock</u> on the garage door.* 2. to shut something in *Don't <u>lock</u> the cat in the house!*
sell	(sel)	to give something away and get money back for it *Jim will try to <u>sell</u> his truck.*
wife	(wīf)	a married woman *Joe and his <u>wife</u> will see a play today.*

Places

Jackson's Island	the place where Huck hides after running away from Pap
New Orleans	a city at the end of the Mississippi River

I Trick Pap and Get Away!

Pap locked Huck in the house so he wouldn't get away.

Preview:
1. Read the name of the story.
2. Look at the picture.
3. Read the sentence under the picture.
4. Read the first two paragraphs of the story.
5. Then answer the following question.

You learned from your preview that Huck had made the house look like
___ a. a pig had been killed.
___ b. a pig had been eaten.
___ c. some robbers had come.
___ d. some friends had been over.

Turn to the Comprehension Check on page 34 for the right answer.

Now read the story.

Read to find out who Huck met on Jackson's Island.

I Trick Pap and Get Away!

Pap came after me for going to school. He got me, too. He made me go up the river with him. He took me to his house in the woods. I heard him lock the door. He kept me locked up.

Then one day, he didn't lock the door. I found a canoe. I pulled it into the woods next to the river. I made the house look like robbers had come. I broke down the door. I got some blood from a pig. I painted the door with some of the pig's blood. Then I painted all over Pap's house. I made it look like I was dead. Maybe then, Pap would not come looking for me.

Then, I ran for the river and my canoe. Later, the people in town looked for my body. I heard them cry. I felt bad, but there warn't nothing I could do. I couldn't stay in Pap's house any more.

I took the canoe to Jackson's Island. At first, I thought I was alone on the island. But then I went looking around. I found Miss Watson's Jim!

I came out of the woods and said, "Hello, Jim!"

I gave him a surprise! He thought I was a dead body who could talk, or some such thing. It took some time to make Jim see I was not dead.

Jim told me an awful story. Miss Watson was going to sell him! She was selling him to some people in New Orleans. Jim didn't want to go. He didn't want to leave his wife and children. So, he ran away!

Jim broke a big rule when he ran away. People would be looking for him. They would lock him up in jail! Jim was my friend. I was not going to let anyone lock him up in jail. My canoe was big. We would run away together!

I Trick Pap and Get Away!

COMPREHENSION CHECK

Choose the best answer.

> **Preview Answer:**
>
> c. some robbers had come.

1. Huck was able to get away when Pap
    ___a. left his keys on the table.
    ___b. forgot to lock the door.
    ___c. went to work.
    ___d. went fishing down by the river.

2. Why did Huck break down the door when he knew it wasn't locked?
    ___a. He wanted to make Pap angry.
    ___b. He wanted to put up a new door.
    ___c. He wanted to make it look like robbers had broken into the house.
    ___d. To let the pig inside

3. Huck put the pig's blood all over the house. He wanted Pap to think that
    ___a. the blood was Huck's.
    ___b. Huck had thrown a party.
    ___c. Huck had painted the house.
    ___d. Huck had cooked a pig for dinner.

4. When the people in town heard about the blood at Pap's house,
    ___a. they went over to clean up the house.
    ___b. they thought the robbers had thrown Huck's body into the river.
    ___c. they laughed at the story.
    ___d. they didn't believe Pap.

5. Huck had taken a canoe to
    ___a. Miss Watson's house.
    ___b. New Orleans.
    ___c. Jackson's Island.
    ___d. Jim's Island.

6. On Jackson's Island, Huck went looking.
    ___a. for treasure.
    ___b. to see if anyone else was around.
    ___c. for a better canoe.
    ___d. for some friends to play with.

7. Jim was very surprised to see that Huck
    ___a. was alive.
    ___b. had come to visit.
    ___c. knew how to paddle a canoe.
    ___d. knew how to fish.

8. Huck had found out that Jim
    ___a. had run away, too.
    ___b. wanted to leave his wife and children.
    ___c. was going to sell Miss Watson.
    ___d. wanted to go to jail.

9. Another name for this story could be
    ___a. "Jim Breaks the Law."
    ___b. "Jim's Awful Story."
    ___c. "Huck's Great Trick."
    ___d. "Alone On Jackson's Island."

10. This story is mainly about
    ___a. meeting a friend on Jackson's Island.
    ___b. killing a pig.
    ___c. Jim running away from Miss Watson.
    ___d. a smart boy who tricks everyone so he can get away from a mean and angry man.

Check your answers with the key on page 67.

I Trick Pap and Get Away!

VOCABULARY CHECK

came	door	pig	some	would

I. Sentences to Finish

Fill in the blank in each sentence with the correct key word form the box above.

1. Mother will give us _____ ice cream after dinner.

2. My brother asked me if I _____ help him rake the yard.

3. My grandmother _____ to visit us yesterday.

4. I shut the gate so the _____ would not run away.

5. When Johnny opened the _____ , he let the cold air inside.

II. Using The Words

On the lines below, write five of your own sentences using the key words from the box above. Use each word once, drawing a line under the key word.

1. _____

2. _____

3. _____

4. _____

5. _____

Check your answers with the key on page 70.

A Family Takes Me In

PREPARATION

Key Words

one	(wun)	a single person or thing *There was <u>one</u> child in the family.*
took	(tŭk)	past tense of take; to have taken something *Linda <u>took</u> the bus into town.*
very	(ver´ē)	much; greatly *My grandmother and I were <u>very</u> happy to see each other again.*
water	(wô´tər)	the liquid that makes rain; oceans and rivers are water *I like to drink cold <u>water</u> on a hot day.*
wet	(wet)	covered with water *Don't walk on the kitchen floor when it is <u>wet.</u>*

A Family Takes Me In

Necessary Words

care   (kãr)

1. to watch over
   I'll take care of your dog while you are away.
2. like; love
   Tony cares very much for his wife and family.

fight   (fīt)

to be very angry and try to hurt others; to hit with one's hands.
   There was a fight at the ball game last night.

float   (flōt)

to stay on top of water
   The logs will float down the river.

gun   (gun)

a weapon that shoots bullets
   The hunter killed the deer with his gun.

quiet   (kwī´ət)

making little or no noise
   Please be quiet when I'm trying to read.

raft   (raft)

a boat made of logs or boards
   We made our way down the river in the raft.

steamboat   (stēm´bōt´)

a boat moved by steam
   The steamboat brought goods and food into the town.

Slang of the Day

Ol'   old

A Family Takes Me In

The steamboat crashed right into their canoe!

Preview: 1. Read the name of the story.
2. Look at the picture.
3. Read the sentence under the picture.
4. Read the first paragraph of the story.
5. Then answer the following question.

You learned from your preview that Jim
___ a.   cried out for Huck many times.
___ b.   jumped into the water to save Huck.
___ c.   could not be found anywhere.
___ d.   took off his wet clothes.

Turn to the Comprehension Check on page 40 for the right answer.

Now read the story.

Read to find out what happened to Jim.

A Family Takes Me In

Well, one night Jim and I floated down the river in the canoe. A big steamboat came at us. It did not see us. It broke right through our canoe! Jim and I jumped into the water. The steamboat went right over me. When I came up, I couldn't see Jim. I cried out for Jim many times. But I didn't hear anything back. I felt awful. I got out of the water. All my clothes were wet. I ran to a house that I saw in the woods.

The family took me in. They gave me some of their children's clothes. I took off my wet things. They liked me and took good care of me.

I didn't tell them about Jim. Maybe he wasn't dead. I would keep quiet. Then no one would go looking for him. I cared a lot for Jim.

One day, I found Jim in the woods! I was so happy to see him. Jim told me he had made a raft. Now we could go up the river again!

The next day was awful. The one family who took care of me did not get along with another family. One day the families began a fight! They had guns. They took the guns into the woods. Then, I heard the sound of the guns. It was a long fight. Many people were dead. It was awful. I was very sorry. These people were good to me. But, I never went back to their house again.

I ran right for Jim in the woods. We took off for the river faster than anything. When we got out on the water, we didn't talk much. It's good floating quietly on a raft. The sky is your roof. The clean smell of the wind was good. Ol' Jim and I took a long rest.

A Family Takes Me In

COMPREHENSION CHECK

Choose the best answer.

Preview Answer:

c. could not be found anywhere.

1. The crash on the river took place
   ___a. in the morning.
   ___b. at noon.
   ___c. at night.
   ___d. on Sunday.

2. The steamboat hit the canoe because
   ___a. the canoe didn't belong on the river at night.
   ___b. it was dark and it couldn't be seen.
   ___c. the men on the steamboat were playing a game.
   ___d. no one was in the steamboat.

3. First, Huck and Jim floated down the river in their canoe. Then a steamboat broke through the canoe. Next, Huck and Jim
   ___a. cried out in the night.
   ___b. ran into the woods.
   ___c. fixed their canoe.
   ___d. jumped into the water.

4. At the house in the woods, the family gave Huck
   ___a. a. birthday cake.
   ___b. some of their children's toys.
   ___c. some of their children's clothes.
   ___d. a hot bowl of soup.

5. Huck changed into the children's clothes because
   ___a. his clothes were torn.
   ___b. his clothes were wet.
   ___c. his clothes were too bright.
   ___d. his clothes were too tight.

6. Huck did not tell the family about
   ___a. the steamboat.
   ___b. the broken canoe.
   ___c. Jim.
   ___d. Jim's family.

7. Huck didn't tell the family about Jim because
   ___a. if Jim was still alive, he didn't want him to get caught.
   ___b. he wanted it to be his secret.
   ___c. they wouldn't have believed him anyway.
   ___d. they may have asked Huck to go away.

8. Huck ran to the woods to find Jim. Then they took off for the river. Huck wanted to
   ___a. do some fishing.
   ___b. go hunting.
   ___c. get away from the fighting families.
   ___d. go shopping.

9. Another name for this story could be
   ___a. "The Floating Raft."
   ___b. "Running from Danger."
   ___c. "The Broken Canoe."
   ___d. "Family Night."

10. This story is mainly about
    ___a. the troubles Huck and Jim find along the river.
    ___b. two families that fight all the time.
    ___c. how Jim got lost in the river.
    ___d. the clean smell of the wind.

Check your answers with the key on page 67.

A Family Takes Me In

VOCABULARY CHECK

one	took	very	water	wet

I. Sentences to Finish

Fill in the blank in each sentence with the correct key word from the box above.

1. I was _____ happy to find my lost dog.

2. Father _____ me to see a show.

3. My coat was _____ from the rain.

4. I can have _____ piece of candy every day.

5. I give the plants some _____ every week.

II. Use the words from the box above to fill in the puzzle. Use the meanings below to help you choose the right answer.

Across

1. covered with water
3. a single person or thing
4. much; greatly

Down

1. liquid that makes rain
2. to have taken something

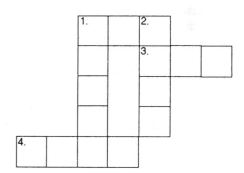

Check your answers with the key on page 70.

This page may be reproduced for classroom use.

The Duke and the King

PREPARATION

Key Words

back   (bak)   something that is away from a person; behind in space or time
> *I have a lot of friends <u>back</u> <u>in</u> my old neighborhood.*

boy   (boi)   a male child
> *The little <u>boy</u> cried when his truck broke.*

just   (just)   only
> *I can't give you more cookies because I <u>just</u> have one left.*

other   (uŦH´ər)
1. that which is left
   > *I'll have this peach and you can have the <u>other</u> one.*
2. different
   > *I got a bike for Christmas. My brother got some <u>other</u> toy.*

way   (wā)
1. a form of doing something; method
   > *Can you show me the <u>way</u> to do this math problem?*
2. one's wish; will
   > *My little sister always wants to have her own <u>way</u>.*

The Duke and the King

Necessary Words

runaway   (run´ a´ wā´)   a person or animal that runs away
                          The <u>runaway</u> horse was never found again.

rope   (rōp)   a strong line or cord
                          Dan tied the dog to the tree with some <u>rope</u>.

sign   (sīn)   something written for all to see
                          The <u>sign</u> in front of Mr. Smith's store said it was closed.

People

Duke of Bridgewater   is a robber and not really a duke.

King of France   is also a robber and not really a king.

Slang of the Day

dats   that's

den   then

dese   these

doan'   don't

mo'   more

reckon'   think

rapscallion   was known as a person who made a living tricking others

The Duke and the King

One morning Huck went into the woods to look for food.

Preview:
1. Read the name of the story.
2. Look at the picture.
3. Read the sentence under the picture.
4. Read the first two paragraphs of the story.
5. Then answer the following question.

You learned from your preview that the duke and the king were
___ a. very important people.
___ b. running through the woods looking for food.
___ c. Pap's kind of people.
___ d. Huck's good friends.

Turn to the Comprehension Check on page 46 for the right answer.

Now read the story.

Read to find out what Jim thinks about the duke and the king.

The Duke and the King

One morning I looked for food. Two men came running through the woods. Some other people were running after them. I knew what that was like! I told the men they could come with us.

One man said he was the Duke of Bridgewater. The other man was quiet. Later, he said he was the King of France. It didn't take me long to know that these men warn't no kings or dukes. I could tell they were making up stories. But I never said nothing. I knew this from Pap. There was a good way to live with Pap's kind of people. That was to let them have their own way.

They asked a lot about Jim. Why did we go up the river in the night? Why did we sleep in the day? I made up a good story.

"Jim is my slave, and I am just a boy. If someone sees us, they might take Jim away from me," said Huck.

The duke had a plan for us to get around in the day. He made up a sign. It said Jim was a runaway.

"This is good," said the duke. "People will see Jim. We will pretend to be taking him back home."

When anyone came around, the duke would put the rope around Jim. Jim didn't like the rope.

He didn't like the sign.

One morning he said, "Boy, does you reckon' we going to run across mo' kings?"

"No," I says. "I reckon' not."

Says he, "Dat's all right, den. I doan' mind just one king, but dat's enough. Huck, dese kings is right rapscallions!"

"I hear all kings is mostly rapscallions," said Huck.

Some nights Jim would sit quiet. I knew why. It was Jim's family back home. He wasn't happy about being so far from home. He cared for his wife and children. He was an awfully good man.

The Duke and the King

COMPREHENSION CHECK

Choose the best answer.

1. Huck met up with the duke and the king as he
   ___a. ran through the woods.
   ___b. looked for Jim.
   ___c. looked for food.
   ___d. was fishing.

2. Huck knew that these men were no "dukes" or "kings" by
   ___a. the way they dressed.
   ___b. the things they talked about.
   ___c. the way they laughed.
   ___d. the way they ate their food.

3. Why did Huck make up a story about Jim?
   ___a. Huck didn't want the men to know what they were up to.
   ___b. Huck liked to make up stories.
   ___c. Jim asked Huck to make up a story.
   ___d. Huck wanted the duke to make a sign for Jim.

4. The duke made a sign for Jim. The sign said that Jim
   ___a. was never to run away.
   ___b. was very hungry.
   ___c. was just a boy.
   ___d. was a runaway.

5. When anyone came around, the duke
   ___a. would chase them away.
   ___b. would run into the woods.
   ___c. would put the rope around Jim.
   ___d. would put the rope around Huck.

6. Jim
   ___a. did not like the sign.
   ___b. didn't like Huck anymore.
   ___c. wanted Huck to wear the sign.
   ___d. wanted Huck to paint the sign.

7. Huck and Jim
   ___a. liked the duke and the king.
   ___b. did not like the duke and king very much.
   ___c. told the duke and the king to go away.
   ___d. cooked dinner for the duke and the king.

8. Some nights Jim would sit quiet and think about
   ___a. Miss Watson.
   ___b. Pap.
   ___c. The Widow Douglas.
   ___d. his wife and children.

9. Another name for this story could be
   ___a. "Jim's New Sign."
   ___b. "King of France."
   ___c. "Meeting the Rapscallions."
   ___d. "Taking Jim Home."

10. This story is mainly about
    ___a. how much Jim misses his family.
    ___b. Huck and Jim meeting up with Pap's kind of people.
    ___c. why Huck and Jim would sleep in the day.
    ___d. going up the river at night.

Check your answers with the key on page 67.

The Duke and the King

VOCABULARY CHECK

back	boy	just	other	way

I. Sentences to Finish

Fill in the blank in each sentence with the correct key word from the box above.

1. I know I can find a better _____ to do the job.

2. Tim got lost when he took the wrong road. He should have taken the _____ road.

3. If you _____ give me one more try, I know I can win the race.

4. The new _____ in school is very smart.

5. I found my lost dog and brought him _____ home.

II. Matching

First, unscramble the letters in Column A to spell out the key words. Then, match the key words with the right meaning in Column B by drawing a line.

Column A

1. yaw   _____

2. stuj   _____

3. thero   _____

4. ybo   _____

5. acbk   _____

Column B

a. a male child

b. away from a person; behind in space or time

c. a form of doing something; method

d. only

e. that which is left; different

Check your answers with the key on page 71.

This page may be reproduced for classroom use.

Huck Tricks the Rapscallions

PREPARATION

Key Words

bag (bag) something made of cloth, leather or paper that will hold things
Hand me that __bag__ of popcorn, please.

bed (bed) something to sleep on or rest on
I go to __bed__ at nine o'clock every night.

girl (gėrl) a young female
The __girl__ sat under a tree and played with her dolls.

letter (let´ər) a written message
A __letter__ came from an old friend that says she's coming to visit.

uncle (ung´kəl) brother of someone's father or mother
__Uncle__ Jack loves to take me to baseball games.

Huck Tricks the Rapscallions

Necessary Words

coffin (kô´fin) a box in which a dead person is put to be buried
The coffin was placed into the ground.

end (end) last; the last part
I didn't like the end of the story.

plan (plan) a way of doing something that has been thought out ahead of time
I plan to visit my sister this summer.

real (rēl) actual or true; not imagined
John bought a real diamond ring for his wife.

Slang of the Day

callin' calling

Huck Tricks the Rapscallions

The duke and the king take money for their new show.

Preview:
1. Read the name of the story.
2. Look at the picture.
3. Read the sentence under the picture.
4. Read the first paragraph of the story.
5. Then answer the following question.

You learned from your preview that the duke and king
___ a. put on shows that made the people happy.
___ b. sometimes left town before doing a show.
___ c. made many people rich.
___ d. had no money to put on a show.

Turn to the Comprehension Check on page 52 for the right answer.

Now read the story.

Read to find out about Huck's good plan.

Huck Tricks the Rapscallions

The duke and the king liked to put on shows. We went to many towns where they would do a show. They made lots of money doing that. Sometimes they would take the money and then leave town — before doing the show! That made a lot of people angry!

In one town, the king found out that a man was dead. The man was the father of three girls. The man would be put in a coffin the next day. The king asked many questions. Then he began talking to the duke. I knew what was coming next!

We went to the girls' house. The duke and the king said that the dead man was their brother. The king and the duke cried very hard. The girls thought they were telling the truth. The girls looked sorry. They asked us to come into the house. They called the duke and the king "uncle."

One girl gave the king a letter. The letter said that the girls would get all of their father's money. That made the girls rich! The girls asked the duke and the king to take care of their bag of money. I knew that would be the end of the money!

I went to bed. I needed a plan to get the money. I could not let these men trick the girls! I got up in the night. I found the bag of money! I hid the money in the coffin. No one would look for it there! Then I went back to bed.

Later, I told one of the girls about the duke and king and where I put the money. But I made her keep quiet about it. We had to watch for just the right time! Then we could put these "uncles" in jail. It was a good plan. It just didn't work!

You see, another man came into town. They said they were the dead man's *real* brothers. Everyone in town was angry! There was a lot of shouting. Some people were callin' for ropes. Then, someone found the bag the money. I ran away real fast to Jim.

But the king and the duke got away, too! They found Jim and me. They began looking at Jim and talking soft. Jim and I knew they were up to no good.

Huck Tricks the Rapscallions

COMPREHENSION CHECK

Choose the best answer.

1. The duke and king put on shows because
   ___a. it made them feel good.
   ___b. it made other people happy.
   ___c. Huck had asked them to.
   ___d. it made them lots of money.

2. Sometimes the duke and king would have to leave town
   ___a. singing.
   ___b. in a bus.
   ___c. in a hurry.
   ___d. on a train.

3. The duke and the king were
   ___a. very kind men.
   ___b. fun to have around.
   ___c. always poor.
   ___d. robbers.

4. The duke and king went to the dead man's house to
   ___a. help the girls.
   ___b. visit their brother.
   ___c. put on a show.
   ___d. try and get the dead man's money.

5. One girl gave the king a letter. It said that
   ___a. the girls would get all of their father's money.
   ___b. Huck would get all of the money.
   ___c. the duke and the king should have the money.
   ___d. the money should be put into a bag.

6. Huck went to bed to
   ___a. get some sleep.
   ___b. trick the girls.
   ___c. think of a plan to help the girls.
   ___d. hide the money.

7. Huck hid the money in
   ___a. a cookie jar.
   ___b. the duke's bed.
   ___c. a different bag.
   ___d. the dead man's coffin.

8. How did everyone learn that the duke and king were not telling the truth?
   ___a. When the dead man's real brothers came into town
   ___b. When Huck told everyone the truth
   ___c. When Jim told everyone the truth
   ___d. When they were caught taking the money

9. Another name for this story could be
   ___a. "The King Gets a Letter."
   ___b. "A Dead Man's Coffin."
   ___c. "Huck Saves the Girls' Money."
   ___d. "A Bag of Money."

10. This story is mainly about
   ___a. Huck trying to "jail" two men who were up to no good.
   ___b. hiding money.
   ___c. leaving money to your children.
   ___d. a letter to the king.

Check your answers with the key on page 67.

Huck Tricks the Rapscallions

VOCABULARY CHECK

bag	bed	girl	letter	uncle

I. Sentences to Finish

Fill in the blank in each sentence with the correct key word from the box above.

1. Sometimes my brother gets into my _____ at night.

2. Mother asked me to send a _____ to Grandmother.

3. My _____ Phil is my dad's brother.

4. Mother has two children. One _____ and one boy.

5. Jerry helped his father put leaves in the _____ .

II. Making Sense of Sentences

Put a check next to YES if the sentence makes sense. Put a check next to NO if the sentence does not make sense.

	YES	NO
1. A <u>letter</u> is hard to look at	_____	_____
2. An <u>uncle</u> can be found in a big box.	_____	_____
3. I left my <u>bag</u> of lunch on the bus.	_____	_____
4. The <u>girl</u> was glad to have a new friend.	_____	_____
5. Tim makes up his <u>bed</u> every morning.	_____	_____

Check your answers with the key on page 71.

This page may be reproduced for classroom use.

A New Name For Huck

PREPARATION

Key Words

as   (az)   the last drink was not as good as the first drink; the last book was not as good as the first one.
> *I will do the work as fast as I can.*

being   (bē´ing)   to be right now
> *I like being a part of the game.*

feet   (fēt)   more than one foot
> *Jim's new shoes made his feet hurt.*

road   (rōd)   a path to travel on
> *The road went past a little duck pond.*

walked   (wôkt)   past tense of walk; to have gone somewhere on foot
> *Kathy walked to school every day.*

A New Name For Huck

Necessary Words

cousin (kuz´n) the son or daughter of one's uncle or aunt
Jill's <u>cousin</u> will visit on Sunday.

hug (hug) put the arms around and hold close
Dan's father gave him a big <u>hug</u> when he got off the plane.

spirit (spir´it) a ghost or fairy
It is said that a <u>spirit</u> lives in the old lady's house.

sold (sōld) to have given up for money
Dad <u>sold</u> his old truck last week.

townspeople (tounz´pē´pl) the people of a town
The <u>townspeople</u> ran the thief out of town.

People

Sally Phelps is Tom Sawyer's Aunt Sally.

Slang of the Day

if'n even if

yes'm yes, ma'am (madam)

tarred and feathered A long time ago, people would put tar and feathers on a person who had done something very wrong. It was very, very hard to get the tar and feathers off. To be tarred and feathered brought great shame to one's family.

A New Name For Huck

Huck just had to find his friend Jim!

Preview: 1. Read the name of the story.
2. Look at the picture.
3. Read the sentence under the picture.
4. Read the first paragraph of the story.
5. Then answer the following question.

You learned from your preview that when Huck went into town,
___ a.   Jim ran away.
___ b.   Jim was robbed.
___ c.   Jim was sold.
___ d.   Jim sat down and cried.

Turn to the Comprehension Check on page 58 for the right answer.

Now read the story.

Read to find out how Mrs. Phelps surprises Huck!

A New Name For Huck

The duke told me to go into town one day. When I got back, I heard some people talking. A runaway slave had been sold. I knew who that was. The duke and king sold Jim when I was gone. I just sat down and cried. I cried very hard. I just had to find Jim!

I walked around town. I heard two men talking about the runaway slave. When I heard he was at the Phelps' farm, I ran. I ran as fast as my feet could go. I'd had it with that duke and king! Later, I heard they got tarred and feathered by the townspeople. I didn't feel sorry for those men. Jim was my friend. Selling him was an awful thing to do! The duke and king just warn't no good!

I walked up the road to the Phelps' house. A woman came running out the door. A lot of children came running, too.

"I haven't seen you in a very long time," said the woman. "It's you at last!" She looked at me real hard. "Ain't it?" she asked.

I came out with a "Yes'm" before I thought. "Call me Aunt Sally!" she said. She gave me a hug. Then she began to cry. "Children!" she said at last. "It's your cousin Tom Sawyer!"

I near fell off my feet. Everyone was happy about me being there. They gave me lots of hugs. I was happy to pretend being Tom Sawyer.

Then I thought about when the *real* Tom Sawyer would come. I had to get to Tom and tell him my story.

Later, I walked down the road. I found Tom. He had come a long way to see his Aunt Sally. And was I ever a surprise to him! He thought I was a spirit. But then I told him about me and Jim. And how Aunt Sally had Jim locked up out back.

Tom said he'd help me. He said to keep pretending I was Tom. He would pretend to be Sid, Tom's brother.

Aunt Sally was awful nice to us. She gave us the same bedroom. That was good. We had to think up a great plan. We had to save Jim!

A New Name For Huck

COMPREHENSION CHECK

Choose the best answer.

1. Huck cried when he found out that
   ___a. Jim had gone fishing without him.
   ___b. the duke and the king had left town.
   ___c. the duke and the king had been tarred and feathered.
   ___d. Jim had been sold.

2. Huck learned that Jim was
   ___a. at Tom's house.
   ___b. at Tom's aunt's house.
   ___c. out shopping.
   ___d. hiding out in the next town.

3. The duke and king had sold Jim to
   ___a. get money.
   ___b. get Huck angry.
   ___c. help Mrs. Phelps.
   ___d. make Jim happy.

4. First, Huck found out that Jim was gone. Then he ran to find Jim. Next,
   ___a. he walked up the road to the Phelps' house.
   ___b. he found Jim down by the river.
   ___c. he gave Aunt Sally a hug.
   ___d. he played with his cousins.

5. Aunt Sally thought that Huck was
   ___a. Mr. Phelps.
   ___b. her cousin.
   ___c. her missing boy.
   ___d. Tom Sawyer.

6. Huck was happy to pretend he was Tom Sawyer. But he was afraid of what would happen when
   ___a. the Widow found out.
   ___b. Jim found out.
   ___c. the real Tom Sawyer would come.
   ___d. Sid found out.

7. When Tom Sawyer met Huck down the road, he thought
   ___a. he was in the wrong town.
   ___b. he was seeing a spirit.
   ___c. Huck was his brother, Sid.
   ___d. Huck was sick.

8. Aunt Sally had Jim
   ___a. rake the leaves.
   ___b. paint the barn.
   ___c. locked up in the bedroom.
   ___d. locked up out back.

9. Another name for this story could be
   ___a. "Jim Runs Away."
   ___b. "Aunt Sally's Farm."
   ___c. "Tom's Many Cousins."
   ___d. "Huck's Big Secret."

10. This story is mainly about
    ___a. Huck trying to save his good friend Jim.
    ___b. Huck trying to be like Tom Sawyer.
    ___c. Aunt Sally buying Jim.
    ___d. the duke and king getting tarred and feathered.

Check your answers with the key on page 67.

A New Name For Huck

VOCABULARY CHECK

as	being	feet	road	walked

I. Sentences to Finish

Fill in the blank in each sentence with the correct key word from the box above.

1. Laura's dress is not _____ nice_____ mine.

2. Jim's _____ get cold when he plays in the snow.

3. We took the wrong _____ and we got lost.

4. I _____ to the store to get some milk.

5. Donna was happy_____ the star of the show.

II. Word Search

All the words from the box above are hidden in the puzzle below. They may be written from left to right, or up and down. As you find each word, put a circle around it. One word, that is not a key word, has been done for you.

```
A   F   U   P   Z   W   X
F   E   X   R   O   A   D
B   E   I   N   G   L   F
V   T   S   W   A   K   Y
W   O   R   D   M   E   A
A   S   T   E   E   D   Z
```

Check your answers with the key on page 70.

This page may be reproduced for classroom use.

Nothing More to Write

PREPARATION

Key Words

better	(bet´ər)	more good; more excellent *A truck is <u>better</u> than a car for carrying wood.*
off	(ôf)	away; away from *I am running <u>off</u> to the store now.*
put	(pu̇t)	place or lay something *<u>Put</u> the toys in the toy box.*
soon	(sün)	in a short time *Dinner will be ready <u>soon</u>.*
think	(thingk)	making an idea in the mind *I <u>think</u> that puzzle will be easy.*

Nothing More to Write

Necessary Words

bullet	(būl´it)	a piece of lead or steel shot from a gun *The <u>bullet</u> hit the man in the arm.*
danger	(dān´gər)	chance of harm *Tom knew the <u>danger</u> in playing in the street.*
dig	(dig)	use hands or tools to make a hole in the ground *If I put a bone in the ground, my dog will <u>dig</u> it up.*
doctor	(dok´tər)	a person who knows how to take care of the sick *Mother called the <u>doctor</u> when Mary got sick.*
enough	(i nuf´)	as many as needed *We had <u>enough</u> players for the game.*
free	(frē)	not a slave; loose *Our dog is <u>free</u> to run in the yard.*
rat	(rat)	an animal like a mouse, but larger *We found a dead <u>rat</u> in the street.*
snake	(snāk)	a long, crawling reptile *When Mother saw a <u>snake</u> in the grass, she ran!*
spider	(spī´dər)	a small animal with eight legs and no wings *Robert found a <u>spider</u> and put it in a jar.*
steal	(stēl)	take something that does not belong to one *If you <u>steal</u> the book, you'll be in big trouble.*

People

Uncle Silas	is Aunt Sally's husband, Mr. Phelps. He is Tom's uncle.

Slang of the Day

heck of a sweat	all worked up; jittery
soft as milk	baby stuff

61

Nothing More to Write

Tom and Huck go to work to free Jim.

Preview: 1. Read the name of the story.
               2. Look at the picture.
               3. Read the sentence under the picture.
               4. Read the first four paragraphs of the story.
               5. Then answer the following question.

You learned from your preview that Tom's plan
___ a.   set Jim free.
___ b.   was as soft as milk.
___ c.   made Jim happy.
___ d.   was full of danger.

Turn to the Comprehension Check on page 64 for the right answer.

Now read the story.

Read to find out about Aunt Sally's big surprise.

Nothing More to Write

I thought we'd steal the key to the door where Jim was. We'd get my raft and run off down the river. Tom wouldn't have it. "That's as soft as milk, Huck!" said Tom. "I have a better way."

He told me his plan. I think *my* plan would have worked. But Tom's plan was much more fun. It was full of danger!

"We will put snakes and spiders in the Phelps' house. I think that will make them let Jim go. If'n they don't let him go, we will put rats in their house!"

Soon, Tom and Huck took off to put their plan to work. The Phelps' were very much afraid. But they did not let Jim go. So Tom had a better plan. They would dig Jim out!

At night, Tom and Huck would dig under the place where Jim was. Soon, the hole was big enough to get Jim out. As soon as Jim came out, we heard the sound of guns! We ran to the raft. Tom got a bullet in him. I think Tom was happy to get a bullet in him.

I got a doctor for Tom. Later, Uncle Silas found me and took me to his house. It was awful not knowing if'n Tom was better.

The next day the doctor and Tom came up the road. Good ol' Jim was with them, too. It was good to know that Tom's leg was better. Soon, Tom's Aunt Polly came in. She knew me! She knew I was not Tom Sawyer. I had to tell the truth.

Aunt Polly put on a happy face. She had a big surprise for me. Miss Watson was dead. And that made Jim a free man!

Soon, Tom began to plan our next adventure. But I didn't have the money for it. Then Tom said my pap didn't get my money. He told me my pap was found dead.

So now there ain't nothing more to write. I'm glad about it too. This book was hard work!

Nothing More to Write

COMPREHENSION CHECK

Choose the best answer.

1. Huck wanted to
    ___a. run off down the river.
    ___b. put snakes and spiders in Jim's place.
    ___c. steal the key to Jim's place.
    ___d. break down the door to Jim's place.

2. Tom told Huck
    ___a. that he had a better plan.
    ___b. that Huck was soft as milk.
    ___c. to steal the key.
    ___d. to get the canoe ready.

3. Huck thought that Tom's plan was better because
    ___a. Tom was smarter.
    ___b. Tom's plans always worked.
    ___c. he liked snakes and spiders.
    ___d. it was more like an adventure.

4. When Tom's plan didn't work, Tom said they would
    ___a. give up.
    ___b. break Jim's door down.
    ___c. shoot Mrs. Phelps.
    ___d. dig Jim out.

5. First Tom and Huck made a hole big enough for Jim. Then Jim came out. Next,
    ___a. Tom got a bullet in him.
    ___b. Uncle Silas found Huck.
    ___c. they heard guns go off.
    ___d. Huck got a doctor for Tom.

6. Tom got a bullet
    ___a. in his head.
    ___b. in his leg.
    ___c. in his arm.
    ___d. in his foot.

7. Huck had to tell the truth about not being Tom Sawyer when
    ___a. Tom's Aunt Polly came to see him.
    ___b. Aunt Polly put on a happy face.
    ___c. the real Sid showed up.
    ___d. when Huck's pap showed up.

8. The person who wrote this story was
    ___a. Uncle Silas.
    ___b. Jim.
    ___c. Tom Sawyer.
    ___d. Huckleberry Finn.

9. Another name for this story could be
    ___a. "Tom Gets a Bullet."
    ___b. "Snakes and Spiders."
    ___c. "Pap is Dead."
    ___d. "Jim Gets Free."

10. This story is mainly about
    ___a. two boys who work hard to set a man free.
    ___b. Aunt Polly's surprise.
    ___c. planning a new adventure.
    ___d. writing a book.

Check your answers with the key on page 67.

This page may be reproduced for classroom use.

Nothing More to Write

VOCABULARY CHECK

better	off	put	soon	think

I. Sentences to Finish

Fill in the blank in each sentence with the correct key word from the box above.

1. Tom thought his bike was _____ than Sam's.

2. Mother asked me to _____ the dishes away.

3. I am happy that dinner will be ready _____ . I am very hungry.

4. Don't you_____ that Mike's car is better than Al's car?

5. I took _____ down the river to do some fishing.

II. Matching

Write the letter of the correct meaning from Column __B__ next to the key word in Column __A__.

Column A	Column B
____1. think	a. more good; more excellent
____2. off	b. in a short time
____3. better	c. place or lay something
____4. soon	d. making an idea in the mind
____5. put	e. away; away from

Check your answers with the key on page 72.

NOTES

COMPREHENSION CHECK ANSWER KEY
Lessons CTR A-41 to CTR A-50

LESSON NUMBER	QUESTION NUMBER										PAGE NUMBER
	1	2	3	4	5	6	7	8	9	10	
CTR A-41	c	b	d	(a)	(d)	a	(c)	d	△b	[a]	10
CTR A-42	(c)	d	d	b	(a)	◇c	a	c	△c	[a]	16
CTR A-43	c	d	(a)	d	a	(c)	(a)	d	△b	[d]	22
CTR A-44	d	c	a	(b)	c	(b)	c	(a)	△d	[a]	28
CTR A-45	b	(c)	(a)	(b)	c	b	(a)	a	△c	[d]	34
CTR A-46	c	b	◇d	c	(b)	c	(a)	(c)	△b	[a]	40
CTR A-47	c	(b)	(a)	d	c	a	(b)	d	△c	[b]	46
CTR A-48	d	(c)	(d)	(d)	a	c	d	a	△c	[a]	52
CTR A-49	d	b	(a)	◇a	d	c	b	d	△d	[a]	58
CTR A-50	c	a	(d)	d	◇c	b	a	(d)	△d	[a]	64

◯ = Inference (not said straight out, but you know from what is said)

◇ = Sequence (order of events in the story)

△ = Another name for the story

▢ = Main idea of the story

NOTES

VOCABULARY CHECK ANSWER KEY

Lessons CTR A-41 to CTR A-50

LESSON NUMBER		PAGE NUMBER

41   HUCK AND THE WIDOW DOUGLAS   11

I.   1. give
2. but
3. she
4. that
5. about

II.

42   JIM AND THE WITCHES   17

I.   1. got
2. then
3. his
4. him
5. had

II.   1. NO
2. NO
3. YES
4. NO
5. YES

43   PLAYING ROBBERS   23

I.   1. children
2. all
3. when
4. they
5. woman

II.   1. c
2. d
3. b
4. e
5. a

VOCABULARY CHECK ANSWER KEY

Lessons CTR A-41 to CTR A-50

LESSON NUMBER

PAGE NUMBER

44 A VISIT FROM PAP

29

I. 1. again
2. who
3. so
4. hear
5. hand

II.

H	Z	P	W	H	O	T	S
E	W	X	X	A	N	O	N
A	G	A	I	N	H	J	A
R	I	B	C	D	K	O	P
G	E	E	V	F	U	S	N
Y	N	G	E	A	R	V	A
S	T	V	F	O	Q	Y	O
O	K	L	L	W	R	X	W

45 I TRICK PAP AND GET AWAY!

35

I. 1. some
2. would
3. came
4. pig
5. door

46 A FAMILY TAKES ME IN

41

I. 1. very
2. took
3. wet
4. one
5. water

II.

¹W	E	²T		
A		³O	N	E
T		O		
E		K		
⁴V	E	R	Y	

70

VOCABULARY CHECK ANSWER KEY

Lessons CTR A-41 to CTR A-50

**LESSON
NUMBER**

**PAGE
NUMBER**

47 THE DUKE AND THE KING 42

I.
1. way
2. other
3. just
4. boy
5. back

II.
1. way
2. just
3. other
4. boy
5. back

a. a male child
b. away from a person; behind in space or time
c. a form of doing something; method
d. only
e. that which is left; different

48 HUCK TRICKS THE RAPSCALLIONS 48

I.
1. bed
2. letter
3. Uncle
4. girl
5. bag

II.
1. NO
2. NO
3. YES
4. YES
5. YES

49 A NEW NAME FOR HUCK 54

I.
1. as, as
2. feet
3. road
4. walked
5. being

II.

A	F	U	P	Z	W	X
F	E	X	R	O	A	D
B	E	I	N	G	L	F
V	T	S	W	A	K	Y
W	O	R	D	M	E	A
A	S	T	E	E	D	Z

VOCABULARY CHECK ANSWER KEY

Lessons CTR A-41 to CTR A-50

I.
1. better
2. put
3. soon
4. think
5. off

II.
1. d
2. e
3. a
4. b
5. c